A Queen's Heart

Poetry Anthology

Volume 1

Rian N. Jenkins

ISBN: 978-1-7353316-0-7

Photography by Vic Weaver Photography

Cover Designed by Naomi Moore of RedFoxx Designs

WaveGraphix, LLC

Edited by Tamika L. Sims of Get Write with Tamika, LLC

Published by Rian N. Jenkins

Crowned By Nichele, LLC

For information on the content of this book, email

crownedbynichele@gmail.com

www.riannjenkins.com

WrightStuf Consulting, LLC

Columbia, SC

www.wrightstuf.com

Printed in the United States of America

Other Projects

A Queen's Anthem
(Poetry Anthology Volume II)

Future Projects

The Reverse Ya Novel Series

This book is dedicated to my parents, Barbara M-J Reaves and the late Leonard Jenkins.

Thank you for always supporting and encouraging me.

I couldn't be here and do what I do well without you!

Love you forever and always!

Miss you eternally, Daddy!

Acknowledgments

God has endowed me with the gift of writing so I must thank Him for trusting me with this gift. My life would be meaningless without Him loving me. I have been writing since I was 12 and this is one gift I never lost sight of. It has evolved over the years through His grace and mercy.

My parents, Ms. Barbara Reaves and the Late Leonard Jenkins have always been supportive of me. Truly this gift is a blessing and inherited through my mother who has been a perfect example. Her words always captured an audience. I remember one time when they traveled to Charlotte from Columbia to see me perform in an open mic event. Thanks for always being there and loving me unconditionally.

Joshua Jenkins, my son, has been my biggest cheerleader. Before publishing this book and watching others publish theirs, he would ask, *"Mommy, when are you going to publish your book?"* When I would share my poetry with him or he would watch my performance, he would say *"Great job!"* With his awesome, intelligent mind, he is able to give me feedback on my poetry and help me when I am practicing. He is also my muse, so I appreciate the inspiration, JJ.

Thanks to those family members who have always been

supportive, especially my Aunt Mary Mungin, who became very excited when I mentioned publishing my first book of poems over 10 years ago.

My spiritual parents, Pastors Herbert and Marcia Bailey of Right Direction Christian Church International, pushed me to maximize every Godly talent while being the best example of Christ on the earth. I am thankful for your relentless teaching for me to be my best.

To all my former and current students, I am thankful that you let me use me as my guinea pigs. As I would read my poetry or bless you with writings that included my poetry, I loved hearing, *"When is your book coming out?"* Your words of encouragement have pushed me.

My first writing mentor, Mrs. Jeanette Gregory Tyson, pushed me to believe in my gift at a different level. She proposed getting me published over 10 years ago and I got scared. She would give me assignments for me to perfect my craft. She saw greatness in me and wanted me to push even further.

My second writing mentor, Jerlean Noble, President of the Columbia Writers Alliance. This is a great group of people to be around if you are seeking to self-publish. The amount of knowledge and information I have gained from her and the members of the group is priceless. Thank you for also helping me edit this project!

My third writing mentor, Ms. Pamela Harris, who has also been my cheerleader from the first day we met. I love how she helped me see that it doesn't matter how good you are as a writer, if you are not hungry enough to cultivate it and do whatever God told you to do with it.

This project is long overdue, and I am glad to share the first of many poetry anthologies with you.

Contents

"A Woman in Bloom"

For you Rian:

I hear you little girl, loud and clear

a pierced heart pounding in my ears

that shy little spirit shedding its fears
stepping into a world of grown up years.

I feel you little girl, the dread, the pain
the knowing your life will never be the same
still finding a love that no one can claim
and true forgiveness in Jesus' name.

I'm here for you little girl, a woman in bloom

no shame in your game, no more, no room

being reshaped, refined, re-groomed
getting ready for the Kingdom coming soon.

Deirdre K Hartsfield © 21 August 2002

Part One

Declaration

A Journey with the Lover of My Soul

Apple of My Eye

You've captured my heart from the very start.

With the thought of you,

before laying eyes on you.

Ever since I fearfully and wonderfully

handcrafted you in My image …

My eyes have been locked on you ever since.

The beauty of your soul shining brightly through

capturing my heart from the very start.

 The rough edges,

life experiences seeking to tarnish your beauty,

do not scare me.

Being the beginning and the end,

already knew what you would endure.

There is no loving you more.

Unconditional, unwavering, my love restores,

giving you all you ever needed, wanted and much more.

You've captured my heart from the very start.

Created you like no one.

Special is an understatement.

Distinct, Extraordinary.

No other you who holds my heart the way you do.

You are mine.

No one else touches my heart like you.

No one else could come close to filling the special spot

you hold in my heart.

Sands seek to outnumber my thoughts of you.

They never come close.

Diamonds and sapphires seek to outshine you.

Jealous, they wish they were created in my likeness.

Ever present, Everywhere, Unchangeable …

I am always with you.

Can't stay away.

Forevermore I am captured.

His Love Melted the Pieces Together

Pain I once felt.

Joy I now feel.

Lust and infatuation

is no longer confused

with the true love I have received.

True love given by a Man on a mission.

Not only redeem my soul

but also warm a heart that was cold.

A heart covered in cuts and bruises.

Marks reminding me of my bad choices

to let this world use and abuse me

while pulling me away from my destiny.

Caught up in deception,

I thought what this world could give was the best.

Yes, it was the best,

BEST COUNTERFEIT --

Cheap imitations of God's abundant blessings.

Amid being raped of my innocence,

Feeling worthless,

I kept hearing a voice telling me I am precious.

I am worth more than this empty feeling.

If I trusted Him,

He would deliver me out of all of it,

giving me all I ever needed and wanted.

I gave this man my heart

along with my mind and soul.

In return …

my pain was healed

true joy was experienced

fulfilling my dreams of finding a love

giving me more than I could ever imagine.

Do I Have Your Attention?

Do you even notice?

I don't smoke or drink.

I don't curse or enjoy the clubs and parties.

I go to church every Sunday.

I even pray every day.

Do you even notice?

I wonder if you notice …

'ol dude over there does smoke and drink.

He does curse and enjoys the clubs and parties.

Doesn't go to church at all.

Top it off, this dude is ballin' hard,

driving a nice, brand new car

Gucci from head to toe

while rocking a Rolex on his arm.

Why am I strugglin' while he is livin' it up?

I thought you are the Shepherd

who would cause me not to want for anything?

Here I am wanting and needing everything.

Do you even notice?

Lord, do you hear me calling?

Yes, son, I hear you calling or shall we call it complaining.

You're ignoring how blessed you truly are,

although you might not have all the material possessions he has.

You are blessed because you sit right with your Dad.

Besides, you do not know what he did to get what he has.

All you see is the outer shell.

You do not see the inner brokenness caused by hell

he tries to hide by dressing in the flyest gear,

driving the smoothest ride.

Yes, I do want you to live life more abundantly

But it is not only about money.

It's about making the most of each moment

by blessing the Kingdom for your atonement.

Do not be concerned with what you see.

Keep your eyes focused on me.

I will give you your heart's desire in due time,

as long as you keep My will for your life on your mind.

Now I have showed you, you are truly blessed

and every blessing is a reminder I notice

One Night Stand

Here I am waiting for your call.

Seeing if you will stick by your promise.

You end up calling late.

Finished with everything, everyone else.

Listening to excuses, accepting your apology.

I love you.

Wanting to make it up to me.

Asking to spend time with me.

I ask you to come over.

I really do miss you.

Yearning to spend time with you.

Opening the door.

Melting my heart .

You are so beautiful.

Passionate hugs and kisses exchanged.

Filling a void.

Holding you in my arms.

The warmth of your touch erasing

any memory of you hurting me.

Remembering only the promises

to love me forever.

Hand in hand, walking to the couch.

Listening to how your day went.

Engulfed in your troubles.

Ignoring your lack of interest in me.

Hearing your sweet voice makes it worth it

revealing the brokenness in your heart,

cries for help.

You forget I know all.

Blinding me isn't an option.

Yet you seek to foolishly cover it up.

Reminding you my love is enough.

Waiting for permission to mend your heart

with my sweet caresses and kisses.

Loving away all the hurt and pain others have given

by diving in your depths and fulfilling every need.

Lying in each other's arms,

dreaming of waking up the next morning

with thoughts of seeing your beautiful face,

feeling your warm embrace.

Opening my eyes to a nightmare.

Nowhere next to me or to be found.

Outside of my presence.

Coming to the realization

again I was used by the one I love so much.

Sadly . . . in all actuality

I knew it was going to happen.

I let it happen.

Love you so much.

Allowing you to hurt isn't an option.

Please realize quick fixes eventually give way.

The only way to completely rid yourself

of the scars on your heart

is to spend more than occasional nights with me.

Must reside at my place every day and night throughout eternity.

Follow My Example

I know how it feels to be . . .

talked about...
    called everything except my name.
Sadly, they were convinced I was the bad guy,
    not the only one who came to speak life.
Threatened...
Betrayed by my closest friend.
All because I went against
    the normal routine of religion.

I know how it feels to be...

Ridiculed…
Spit on…
Humiliated and embarrassed...
    by people who claim to love our Creator.

Literally whipped to a bloody pulp.

Still, I did not give up

Not because

   I knew these afflictions would only last a moment.

Not because

   of the glorious reward I would receive for my obedience.

I kept pushing my way to the cross

   so the will of our Father could be done.

Dreams of Wings (Part One)

Wanting to get away from the drama and madness...
Wanting to go somewhere quiet and peaceful
    where I can relax ...
has me dreaming of wings.

Hearing about people going on violent rampages...
Knowing the world will soon not be a safer place...
Has me dreaming of wings.

When people do not understand me...
But instead of trying to, they misinterpret me...
Calling me names and scandalizing me...
Has me dreaming of wings.

When the world gets too complicated...
I do not feel like dealing with it...
I dream of flying away somewhere far.
Flying to a peaceful destination.

Where there is no stress.

No hate.

Everything is beautiful.

There is no reason to have a negative attitude.

Everyone there is happy.

There is no inequality of any kind.

The sky is always blue

Or when it rains, it rejuvenates everything around including you.

But no place like that exists...

At least on earth.

All I can do is dream ...

'til my Lord grants me some wings.

Dreams of Wings: Used to Dream of Wings (Part Two)

I used to daydream about flying away

to a distant land

to get away from the stress and strife.

Now I hide in my Father's shadow

burying myself in His presence

Surrounding myself with the peace He gives.

Peace surpassing all understanding.

Peace making the raging winds of a storm

feel like a gentle breeze

bringing me relief on a humid day.

In the middle of chaos

A sweet melody plays in my spirit

reminding me I am a daughter of the Most High.

Nothing is formed to hinder me or destroy me shall prosper.

Nothing can defeat me.

I have victory through Christ.

No longer will I puff and pout

when this world tries to wear me down.

I will no longer wish for wings

to carry me away from the trials and tribulations.

I will gladly face the storms

knowing that in everything

God works out for the good of those who love Him.

Knowing after every storm

there is a rainbow that elevates me to a new glory.

Can I Rock the Mic for Jesus?

It's the Anointed Misfit.

Comin' to rip it in the name of Jesus Christ

who is the head of my life.

Because of Him, I was made right in God's sight.

Now I have eternal life,

a personal relationship with the Lover of my soul

who I allow to have control over my destiny.

He knows what's best for me.

Besides my life would be incomplete

without Him guiding me.

Where would I be if the Lord had not saved me

raised me from life that was degrading

failing to give me what I ultimately craved:

Love making all the hurt and pain go away

Love seeing past the mistakes I make

Love never changing

Love loving me for me, appreciating me.

Giving me a purpose and destiny worth living for.

Love never ending

Love never pretending

forever be true to what He was called to do.

I'm so grateful Love found me, chose me

to be a representation of His glory.

Now I can tell everyone

about a King who wants to be their everything.

Fulfilling their dreams by making them kings and queens,

heirs of everything our Father possesses.

They can be a blessing to others

who have not truly experienced who God truly is.

Some of y'all are sleepin' on how excellent He is.

Believe it or not, God is the best thing there is.

Nothing could come close to the love He gives.

Stop fronting, giving God a little something.

Surrender to Him your all.

He wants you to love Him with your whole heart.

Wanting you to experience more than a blessing,

but abundance.

Foolish

Watching water fill a tank

imprisoning me

while desperately

stretching for air

to breathe.

Seeing water creep

slowly over me

noticing a way of escape—

a rope dangling

within my reach.

Instead, I

close my eyes

and allow the water

to overtake me.

Incomprehensible

What is love?

Who are you?

Who am I

who is so undeserving

not worthy of this love?

Yet . . .

you won't take no for an answer

Never do you force what I deem

too lofty for me

to comprehend

Daily moments are snapshots

of what life would be,

if I said yes!

Yes, to your promise to love me,

Eternally.

Again, I ask . . .

What is love?

Who are you?

Who am I

so undeserving

not worthy of this love?

See never was I told or made to believe

I was good enough.

Content with average.

Not understanding

this language you speak of

Royalty is my namesake?

Little 'ol me has a place at your table,

A king's table?

Unfathomable

Satisfied with the scraps

Desiring more

But been told countless times

I am not entitled to success, excellence

Stagnant is the only

potential level

I will experience.

You say you will dispel that myth.

From the beginning,

you bestowed a crown

for me not to wear,

but to exhibit greatness.

Because of you being slain,

descending to hell

to be seated high in Heaven,

 manifesting abundance, life everlasting

to all including me

I don't have to ask . . .

What is love?

You are agape.

Who are you?

You are my dearest father, closest friend.

Who am I

so undeserving?

Being your daughter makes me worthy.

Declaration

Rebellious
is what my Father
told me I need to stop being.
Keep rejecting the Master's plan
has been shoved back and forth
across the table for nearly 15 years.

Cheers come from the stands of hell.
I have chosen to rebel.
Run in the other direction.
Plot my next move to be
bigger and badder than the last.

Ignoring the gash, bruises, scars
All could be healed.
If I kneel and pray
ask for forgiveness while repenting
never again will I forsake you.

I promise you . . .

I want to . . .

I desire to . . .

There's something about being holy.
I would wear my robe temporarily
before getting tired.

Momentary gain is what I settled for.
Forgetting He promises life everlasting,
abundant living.

Un-arming myself.
Choosing not to use the weapons
created only for victory.
Accepting defeat, mediocrity
when royalty flows through my veins.
Denouncing my crown
when it is convenient.
Placing all the knowledge,
scriptures, wisdom, teachings
in what some would deem Pandora's box.

Insane.

Stupid.

Foolish.

I would allow Satan to literally choke the life out of me.

Hyperventilating while disobeying the One who created me.

Saved me by releasing

then giving me a way to escape the devil's grasp.

Restoring oxygen.

Cleaning up the pollutants disillusioning

me into thinking abuse was okay.

Two Faced

Hypocrite --

Expecting others to follow a standard I wouldn't follow

consistently, wholeheartedly.

Pardon me, Devil,

I just had an epiphany

on June 20, 2012.

I can't

I won't

do this anymore.

You laugh.

You heard this before.

Smarter

Wiser

I am reading this to my sisters

who will encourage me to stop rebelling.

Tired of living this lie I am all right.

As I write this, I crucify myself,

the real hindrance in my relationships with Christ

No longer denying the power I have spiritually been awakened to.

Pastor Bailey and Pastor Marcia have performed CPR.

Breathing words resurrecting.

No longer will I be hard headed.

Ignoring the stench of rotting flesh.

Allowing the deceiver to devalue this Master's piece.

I cannot live my life without you, God.

There is no comparison.

I have tasted and saw countless times you are good.

Now refusing the scraps at the table

when you made a buffet available

with all my favorite fixings...

Love that will permeate and save the soul

Generational inheritances experienced in my generation
Power to produce wealth for generations to come
Health immediately felt at the touch of my finger

I am not flipping the script, devil.
Ripping it out of your palms, shredding it then burning it.
Refusing to any longer be associated
with someone who only seeks to kill, destroy and devour

Shall not believe the lie I am not worthy of the God kind of life.

No longer denying the power within.
Letting my light shine so bright, darkness will flee me.

I am an obedient daughter who is done misbehaving

Rebellious I will be to you.
Won't conform to the world's system.
Exercising my dominion.
Helping to expand the Kingdom.
Raising a son who deserves for me to break the curse.
The vicious cycle will not claim my life or my right to possess everything my Father promised me.

Part Two

I Rise to Call You Blessed

Odes to Family

I Rise to Call You Blessed

Words truly cannot express how grateful I am to have you.
You ever gave up on your children
You brought on you a lot of unnecessary stress.

I will attempt to express in words my gratitude
towards a woman of virtue
who willingly unconditionally gives love
making the Father up above smile.
Truly you do your best to do whatever you can
to answer to the call God has given you.

Some cannot share my testimony
of having a mother who never gave up on me.
Faithfully, you stick by while sowing seeds
of wisdom reaping a harvest of strength
carrying me through life's journey.

I take this opportunity to call you blessed.

The beauty you exemplify while displaying the love of Christ.

No one can do the wonderful things you do

in the amazing way that you do it

explaining why God chose you to be

one of the best parents that I now truly cherish.

I do not know where I would be if

you had not allowed the Lord to use you to be my mommy.

I cannot forget the sacrifices you gave.

Wish to repay you with cars, houses, trips around the world.

Lord knows I will fall short of your infinite worth.

Today I promise I will continue

to live a life reflecting the foundation you have laid.

Assuring you your guidance does not go to waste.

Continue to allow the blessings of the Lord to overtake you.

He has truly favored you to endure all you have been through.

Thank you for the discipline you showed your love through spankings, punishment, and long stern talks

Molding this daughter

who takes joy in this moment to call you blessed.

Dedicated to my mother, Barbara Reaves.

Daddy's Girl

As the youngest girl in my daddy's world...

I wanted to have his attention

in every aspect of my existence...

better known as a Daddy's girl.

I used to think I didn't.

My brother, the only boy, youngest child

seemingly his favorite.

Then it hit me,

memories flooding like a dam bursting

to bring life to a thought...

With fathers and sons, fathers and daughters

sports is a bond no one can tear.

For some reason,

I only believed the bond was shared on the couch

through many basketball and football TV viewings.

Now to add to the valley...

I remember him giving me tennis lessons.

No, he wasn't the patient teacher.

What counts is he took me.

I remember waking up early

on a hot summer morning

practicing my 100 meter start on a clay track.

Stopwatch in his hand

pushing me to run harder.

I remember him setting up the video camera at track meets.

Telling me after the race

I should have taken off faster at the corner.

Yes, sports is a bond shared with father son

But this daughter can say she had that same bond with my father.

Most importantly, it wasn't the sports holding us together.

It was his love for his children and wanting us to be successful.

I am a Daddy's girl.

Dedicated to my father, the late Leonard J. Jenkins

Bereavement

Wanting to close my eyes.

Tired and weariness bears heavy on my eyelids

Fear of facing another day without you keeps them open.

Desperately wanting to believe, I am living a nightmare. Needing
to stay awake.

Closing my eyes will make this phantasm real.

Realizing I won't hear your footsteps

downstairs in the morning.

Granted you are in heaven

in glory where no pain exists.

Nevertheless, can't help, but be selfish.

I'd rather be having one of our talks,

just watching sports or a movie

with you sitting on the couch with me.

Don't want to withstand tomorrow; I won't see you.

Discomfort lurks heavy overshadowing comforting peace.

Must be willing to press on,continuing to live out your legacy fulfilling your expectations for me.

Must stay strong for the family --utterances in the bottom of my heart.

Need someone to uplift me, keep me from drowning in my unwillingness to see this as a blessing.

Struggling yet determined to persevere .

Immensely, longing for you here.

Dedicated to my father, the late Leonard J. Jenkins

Wisdom Never Fades

Although you are not physically with us,

the essence of your soul is ingrained in our hearts.

Sharing precious memories, never to be erased.

Obtaining wisdom you spoke into our lives

coming from our Heavenly Father who are now with.

Wisdom speaking truth about life.

Although sometimes we did not always receive

    the incorruptible seed planted in our hearts,

    later we would find ourselves reaping a harvest

    ministering to critical moments in our lives.

I praise God you never ceased to let truth

    spring forth like a wanted rainfall on a humid day.

You never held your tongue

    when it came to sharing encouragement

    pushing us to a higher level of doing our best.

Thank you for exemplifying what it means to be virtuous

who always gave wise counsel.

Even though you are dearly missed,

    although your body is in the grave

    your spirit is shining bright in the holy place

    and here with us are precious memories,

    wisdom that will never fade.

Dedicated to my grandmothers, the late Mary Jenkins-Dent and late Viola Mungin.

Illumination

Her smile illuminated a room.

Her laugh echoed in souls

electrifying the atmosphere

of happiness and cheer.

Contagious to all.

Felt by everyone in her presence.

Heaven sent.

Her children, grands and husband rise to call her blessed.

Fortunate God saw fit

to give them her as a gift

to be forever cherished.

Memories will never be enough.

She will forever live in and through

the ones she impacted.

Her legacy isn't lost.

Captured in daughters

who are mothers

resembling the golden moments

wrapped in wisdom and love

being passed down to multiple

generations

She will live on forever illuminating.

Dedicated to my cousin, the late Renee Wright

My Sister's Keeper

I couldn't let you fall.

Watching your every move.

Remembering how I caught you the last time.

Determined not to let you fall.

When you were singing the solo,

mourning consumed you

to the point of consoling.

Standing up.

Wishing to catch you.

Too far away.

Forced to sit

where people didn't know

my heartache . . .

Seeking to console you

like you did for me.

Glad your mother was there.

On the way to view

her one last time,

I made sure I was there.

I couldn't let you fall.

I would be your strength.

The rock in the time of grief

Assuring you I am here for you

like you were there for me.

Back on Joyce Street …

having you home.

Bragging I have a big sister!

Never forgot when you caught me whimpering.

My friends wouldn't play with me.

Willing to kick me to the curb

like stale garbage.

You marched me right back into the lion's den.

Told them what I wasn't brave enough to utter

All of you ain't no better. . .

. . . Don't you mess with my sister!

Never could I be any more prouder!

Honored, she didn't let me fall into a pity party,

whining over they not hanging with me.

Yeah, they apologized.

more after seeing that Mt. Vernon in your eyes.

Back in Hollywood …

The family friend wasn't up to no good.

Smelling a wolf who looked like a sheep to me.

Demanding him

BACK OFF OR I WILL HURT YOU!

Eyes wide open

Embarrassed, he got checked for his foolishness.

Awkwardness filled the moment.

Putting space in between who I thought was family.

You didn't let me fall for the games.

A big sister

deserves the love and affection

of a litter sister,

who is forever grateful

you didn't let me fall.

Determined to be there every moment.

Again, bereavement brought me to

this promise not to let you fall.

Watching your every move.

Willing to jump to your rescue.

Being vigilant

while you were consoling him.

Strong you are.

Eventually, I knew I had to be stronger.

Waiting, praying, emotions will allow me to stand.

Enduring until the end.

Knowing seeing him one last time

will cause you to fall.

I would be there.

I was right there.

Arms holding you close, loving you.

Consoling you.

I couldn't let you fall.

Watching your every move.

Remembering how I caught you the last time.

Determined not to let you fall.

Dedicated to my sister, Michele Robison

Daddy's Reflection

You are the thunder calming the storm.

Never alarmed; there is a peace about your soul,

reminding me everything is under control.

At first, I thought it was your tone.

Never forget the moment it resonated

you reflect, bear a strong resemblance --

the depth and gentleness, reminding me of our father.

Always made sure we were secure.

Never just about helping out when resources run out.

The best gift is the time spent, pouring into your nephew.

Babysitting when sleep was minimal.

Moving away broke my heart.

Torn apart between being okay with you finding your way yet
wanting you to stay most importantly for him.

My heart has been mended, repaired, and

restored with you, traveling for hours to support.

Showing how proud you are to be his uncle.

Never could truly express the joy felt seeing his chest puff with excitement, "Uncle Mike is in the building."

Representing what a man truly is.

Eternally appreciative of who you are, the support

Love you! Forever and Always.

Dedicated to my brother, Brian M. Jenkins

Distinguished Gentleman

Cool, dapper

With a Stetson, baseball cap, or a Panama Jack hat

A gentle giant with a smile

Making everyone feel welcome.

The patriarch of the Mungin clan

Knowing our land, our history

Deep rooted in your stories

All listen with a drink or two

Or at the dock where the waves rock you into a peace.

By the sea is your sanctuary.

Your haven hooking bliss and victory.

The brother, husband, father, uncle, papa

All roles have us admiring.

Loving

Understanding

Joking

Distinguished gentleman.

Dedicated to my uncle, John Mungin.

Ola's Girls

Style, grace, elegance

Mungin women

exhibit it the best.

Spoiling their children, overindulging their grands.

Making nieces and nephews feel like sons and daughters.

Home cooked meals are perfect, wonderful

drawing many to the table.

Recipes passed down to generations

Shoppers, thrifters, the best storytellers, dancers, givers

Wisdom given regardless if you want to hear it; they know you need it.

The Earth knows them by name.

Grateful they beautify the subdivision, a glimpse of Heaven.

Flowers bow in their presence.

Brims of glory.

Heels firm in the foundation the Lord has built.

People stop and gaze as beauty passes their way.

Confident those are Ola's girls.

Dedicated to my mother and aunts, Audrey Haynes and Mary Mungin

I bleed Geechee (WHERE I'M FROM)

I am from *shelly* beaches, from Piggly Wiggly and bumpy dirt roads.

I am from the three-bedroom homes that always had the sweet smell of biscuits.

I am from the pecan trees, and the oak trees that protect the road.

I am from feasts on holidays like Christmas and Thanksgiving and spades tables and Taboo quarrels, from Aunt Mary and DJ and Mia.

I am from the cookouts ending under the stars, while cracking open crabs.

From Grandma Ola knowing she would lose one of her children in a dream and Grandma Mary never knowing how Daddy paid his way through college.

I am from Christian heritage with strong roots in the AME, Baptist, and United Methodist Church.

I'm from Edisto Beach and Hollywood, red rice with shrimp okra soup.

From the many fights and arguments of family members, we now look back and laugh at Grandma Ola chasing Rea with the rake down to Aunt Eve's house, and Shanta assuring Mia she needs to duck for cover under Grandma's table.

I am from endless photo albums of black and white, color photos, video tapes of us dancing and singing, and memories lingering ... waiting to be passed on to the next generation.

Part Three

A True Definition of a Good Girl

The Fall and Rise of Self-Esteem

A True Definition of a Good Girl

See, I'm a good girl,

but not your average good girl

who is quiet and shy

doesn't say much.

Only tries to smile away

the hurt in this world.

No, I'm that good girl

who has a bold voice

needing to be heard.

The dry bones lying dormant

will finally rise up to their true purpose and calling.

O' yes, I'm a good girl,

but no longer that average good girl

who uses her shy and quiet nature

to cover up she's a really wild girl.

No, I'm that true good girl

who ain't trying to be your girl

or allow you to get close

to even touching this pearl

who is worth more

than you could ever imagine.

Knowing my father

paid a high price to set me free,

I can't let any man be with me

only the one my Father

anointed and appointed to marry me.

No, my only purpose is to be someone's wife.

My ultimate purpose to speak life

to all those who don't know Christ

so they can experience a life

filled with unconditional love from a God who is faithful

and wants them to experience a life that is full

of abundant blessings that will never stop flowing

as long as you don't lose focus.

Truly, I am a good girl,

but no longer that average good girl

who seeks the approval of man

doing whatever she can

to fit into his standards.

No, I'm that good girl

who no longer conforms to this world
only conforms to the One
in whom I live, move, and have my being.
He is the reason why I exist.
His love raised me out of a fiery pit of sin,
into a life where I've discovered
 being with a brother does not define me.

This good girl's definition lies
in the Father who created me.
In His image where there is no imperfection,
only excellence, intelligence.
Fearfully and wonderfully made
beautiful in my Father's time.
Glory shining brightly through.
Outshining all the diamonds in this world
Showing you
what a good girl truly is.

Lois Selah Estelle Speaks (Low Self-Esteem)

Who hasn't noticed or heard about

me?

Scoped out or asked his boys about

or preyed, plotted on

me?

Later approach

me.

Spit game to

me.

Easily impressed

me.

Seduced

me.

into thinking that

I

am worth something.

Compelled

me

to show him

I

felt the same way.

Enticed

me

to let him

hug,

touch,

kiss

fondle

penetrate

me.

Then later watch him leave,

                  never be seen again.

Who hasn't appeared

to be the man of my dreams

who would come to rescue

me?

Give

me

the love

I

have been craving.

Fooled

me

to believe he would never leave

like the last guy.

Who hasn't had his way with,

depreciated?

Left pondering what

I

did wrong to lose him.

All

I

I wanted to be loved by him.

I

was the perfect girlfriend.

I

didn't nag when he wanted

to hang out with his friends,

obtaining numbers of more flings.

I
didn't complain
when he came home late
left behind another's woman's taste
with his kiss g'night.
Each time
I
am more determined to do whatever
I
can to keep the next one.
Put up with
the name-calling,
slapping,
and cheating.
I
need to be loved by him.
Eventually, he will change
give
me
his last name, making
me
glad that

I

stayed.

I

want someone to love

me

False Enhancements

I had a dream.
I was walking through the hospital
Desperately searching for someone
to be willing to make a trade with me.
I ran into a room of a woman
who wanted smaller breasts.
I asked if she would like mine
in exchange for hers?
My ideal cup size.
She obliged
But the doctor wouldn't allow me
to take something that wasn't mine.

As I walked out,
I heard another woman complaining
that her calves were too big.
As I ran into her room,

I realized that they were the right size.

I asked if she would like mine

in exchange for hers.

She obliged

But the doctor wouldn't allow me

to take something that wasn't mine.

As I walked out,

hoping to find a patient

who was not in that doctor's care

But everyone was.

So I decided to sneak in without him being there.

I heard a girl crying to the nurse

that her feet were too wide and short.

I asked if she would like mine

in exchange for hers?

She obliged.

The doctor walked in and said he would not allow me

to take something that wasn't mine.

Disgusted he will not budge.

Maybe if I pleaded with tears in my eyes,

he will change his mind?

"What can I do to make you see that I need these things?"

What can I do to make you see that you don't need anything?

"You don't understand."

Yes, I do understand that you're trying to change yourself into what appears to be more appealing.

Don't you realize that beauty does fade. Your body will change

It seems you are seeking for guys to only see you as a showpiece instead of the beautiful, virtuous woman you were created to be.

"These things will enhance my beauty."

Don't be foolish. It will only add to your appearance.

Besides your beauty is not based on a factor that can be altered at any given minute.

It's about your heart and what flows out of it.

Stop chasing after the image men think that they want

but not serious about it.

Seek to be a woman of intellect who has the attention of one special man who treasures his precious gift.

Nonetheless, seek to be a woman of purpose.

Seeking to establish the Kingdom.

Driven to live out My plan, which is much bigger than getting the attention of man.

A Master's Piece

I am and forever will be, a Master's piece.

No crack

no rust or tarnish

will ever depreciate me.

Decisions may sometimes be

a contradiction

not reflecting

a woman

who is priceless.

Nevertheless,

it doesn't diminish

or make me worthless.

Tear me down

with your words

because I walked around

momentarily without my crown.

I am and forever will be a Master's piece.

Quickly,

I am forgiven.

Repentance frees me

to walk in dominion.

Forgetting the shame.

Only answering to

my true name,

Righteous.

Worthy of every promise

my Father bestowed on me.

Queen, I am.

Forever will be

a representation of His glory.

A walking manifestation of blessings.

My purpose,

my reason for being

is inscribed, engraved in crimson.

Causing this woman to wear

a garment so pure and radiant

The lilies of the fields envy me.

Diamonds, gems, and sapphires of the earth

I wonder how they can outshine me.

I am and forever will be a Master's piece.

No crack

no rust or tarnish

will depreciate me.

Created in my Father's image.

His likeness gives me the boldness

to make this confession.

I am and forever will be a Master's piece.

Naturally Speaking

I feel like a minority...
  not due to my African heritage
  not due to carrying both chromosomes,
    which makes me a woman.

The kinky, curly coils standing tall
        like a crown
  are constantly being denounced as ugly.

How soon do we forget
  before the relaxer
  before the press 'n curl.
our hair was a beautiful halo
  in either cornrows or afros
  lighting up the room with our glow.
Then all of sudden it became
    unmanageable, nappy.

Not silky straight like mainstream culture.

Wrapped up in an ideology,

we have forsaken our identity and

      ostracizing anyone

        who wants to embrace

      her curls and waves

God naturally bestowed on her.

I still have good hair.

Sexy never left my swag.

My beauty has not decreased like stock

'cause you're too caught up or

not bold enough to put the crack pipe down.

Let me be me,

the me God created me to be.

Encourage me or

don't say anything.

Two Sides of The Coin

Determination

In the midst of your

frustration, disappointment, rage, negative criticism …

Have you noticed that I am unfazed?

Desensitized to anything

keeping me from pushing towards the prize.

Blocking out and hurdling any comments

not intentionally boost my esteem.

Knowing you meant to tear me down

only pushes me further to my goal.

Blind Desperation

In the midst of your frustration, disappointment,

rage, negative criticism

Do you notice I am unfazed?

Desensitized to anything

that is supposed to be constructive criticism.

Do you not see the wall that I have built?

Technically, I don't hear you.

Yelling accompanied by the looks conveying hatred.

Unlike the battle of Jericho, my wall won't come tumbling down with a loud shout.

Desperately crave sincerity convincing me that you do believe in me.

Behind the Blinds

Apparently,

I don't know or

maybe

I can't remember.

There is a war,

a FIGHT inside.

Battle for my life.

My mind is consumed,

overwhelmed

with generational curses,

past mistakes

haunting and resurfacing

as present struggles.

My soul is tossed.

Lost, you call me

so teach me.

Don't beat me or

return the same

nasty attitude and

expect my hard shell to melt.

HELP

MINISTER

MENTOR

SMILE

ENCOURAGE ME

with love.

Tell me I am

BEAUTIFUL

INTELLIGENT

ELEGANT

WORTH IT,

lessons I ignored

from my mother or

it was never delivered.

Affection, not appreciated

from my father

or left malnourished due to neglect.

Let's be honest...

the cracks

holes

rust

chipped, dull paint

isn't hard to detect.

Transparent,

brokenness is evident.

Pay attention.

Focus on what is relevant,

something or someone

other than yourself.

Again … HELP!

Haters Motivate Me

Boulders

road blocks,

all of you can

KICK ROCKS.

EAT MY DUST.

You believe

I can't.

I will

defy ALL negativity,

disbelief.

I laugh

in your face

while allowing

you to be

my step stool

PUSHING ME

closer to my dream,

the goal

you said

I would never

accomplish.

HypeMan

Why do I allow

     popular culture

     society

to call a female I hang with

confide in, shed tears with, laughed with,

a hoe, trick, or female dog?

Why do I allow

     the cool crowd

     the industry

to degrade my sister,

who has had my back since the beginning

with a label that's so beneath her?

Royalty runs through our veins.

Nevertheless, I crown her with disgrace and shame

of a name some people in the entertainment industry make it okay

to say.

Is it really okay?

I will slap a brother.

Let those words out due to his anger, frustration.

I will beat a female down.

She wrote or said anyone of those words in the same sentence

with any of my girls' or my name.

As an insult, it is not tolerated.

Well, how can an insult be turned into a compliment

when the same word with the same definition is used?

Why do we allow

    them

    him

    and her

to make us look like fools.

We took the same term causing us to feel defensive

to playfully and unknowingly demote our friends' value

with a name that only depreciates.

Higher Thinking

When I know that I am beautiful...

I am confident in the fact

God fearfully and wonderfully made me in His image

where imperfection does not exist.

This confidence convinces me

no one is superior.

He handcrafted all of us.

There is also no need to be jealous or envious

of anyone who may seem to possess more than me.

Uniqueness is truly a quality of God's body.

I carry my head high,

never allow critics to lower it.

What they utter are opinions—false statements.

Throughout the Book of Truth

I am told that my worth is infinite, priceless.

I am God's.

Don't have to always dress up

Wear make-up.

Boots and jeans with my hair flowing in the wind

Or sneaker and sweats with my hair being hidden by my hat—

The attire does not matter.

Beauty comes from within.

Outer appearance is only a small part of it.

Seeking the approval is not my agenda.

Don't need confirmation.

Don't demand or wait on compliments.

I don't go out of the way to receive attention.

Popular culture doesn't dictate my beauty standard. Solely grounded in my Jesus' thoughts concerning me.

Our Influence

I am a bit disturbed.

Needing my dissatisfaction to be heard.

When I look at the apparel of our young Black queens and princesses,

staring in the face of Marilyn.

Out of all the iconic Black women,

you rock the image of someone who did nothing for you.

Didn't break down any barriers for you like . . .

Sojourner Truth

        Spoke boldly about us being set free.

        Women being treated equally.

           Posing the question still being asked

                Ain't I A Woman?

Josephine Baker

Shaking more than a tailfeather

Shaking down the great walls

Seeking to separate all

Shaking the chains of racial injustice

Standing next to MLK, Jr on the March

on Washington

Shirley Chisolm

Determined and ended up having

the first Black seat in Congress.

Obama wouldn't be without her bid for the

Presidency.

Oprah Winfrey

Capturing an audience of millions.

The first of many more to follow.

Impacting the world with a mic.

Blessing the world beyond belief.

Maybe I should blame

Fashion designers

who never or hardly ever

produce a woman in power

or legendary female

resembling the brown, mocha, chocolate shell.

Our faces are not neatly

folded on shelves, displays or hanging on racks.

Betty Boop and Marilyn

seemingly this generation embraces.

Neglecting faces who resemble their own.

Maybe the lack of representation

of strong ancestral lines

of sisters is attributed

to the belief black doesn't sell.

Only we can change that mindset.

Designing, marketing, selling, buying.

The small business owner will become a major corporation.

All because we want to celebrate our own.

Lena Horne

Wilma Randolph

Dr. Mae Jemison

Maya Angelou

Michelle Obama

Our fashion defines us

Speaks of the boldness

Exhibiting in our strut

Confessing my Black is beautiful.

More than enough.

Dismissing the notion

a woman named Marilyn

had any influence.

Part Four

If I Knew Then What I Know Now

Tales of the Heart

Door Number One

I am apprehensive to let go.

Fear of the unknown…

has me pacing back and forth in a room.

Contemplating, staying or

    entering door number one.

You are behind it, waiting to embrace me.

Anxiety causing your heart

to beat a little faster than normal.

"Will she be mine or

    will this be another time I get it wrong?"

I keep inquiring about the same thing.

Remembering a similar situation

when I let a man have my heart.

He was convinced

we would never be apart.

Later, I crushed his hopes and dreams.

Cold feet drove me back

    to the room of familiarity,

which was perceived as safety and warmth.

Uncertainty of what we could have been

    drove me away from him.

I didn't give it a chance.

Afraid to take the risk.

Now I stand in the same room

facing the same door.

Opportunity knocks with a different beat.

Should I answer?

I want to.

Paralyzed by the cowardice nature

bombarding me with question after question

"What if it doesn't work out?"

"Will our pasts pull us apart?"

"Will our futures separate us even more?"

"Will we continue to make each other happy?"

"Could we continue to embrace each other's faults?"

Then I hear a voice say,

"You won't know if you never open the door at all."

Bruised but not Speechless – Whispers of Strength

You made it easy to walk away.

Thoughts of the past

keep me in a place

of hurt and confusion.

How can the man

who would build me a pedestal

place me gently on top

so he can marvel at the beauty

I am still discovering.

SNATCH me out of my place of worth

while kicking dirt and rocks.

Never stopping to notice

the blood shed flowing with

a steady stream of tears.

Although missing you

has me contemplating

whether or not I should

give you another chance,

my heart hasn't had enough time to heal.

The bruises still ache with pain.

I can't relive those moments again.

Change is not an overnight process.

How do I really know

your apology was sincere

this time?

All these thoughts leave me

in a detrimental state.

Dazed and disturbed…

the man I confide in

bear my soul to

would use my weakness

to build a ledge

to push me off

when the heat was turned on.

The man I would laugh with

and enjoy our conversations would

blow up without warning

over something that was either a misunderstanding or

him not willing to admit I hurt his feelings.

The man I would naively see as an image of greatness,

godly guided your thoughts.

Double-minded, the devil asked you to throw daggers to pierce deep
into this skin you called beautiful.

You made it easy to walk away

with my dignity

crawling slowly to a place of refuge.

Choosing not to dial your number.

Missing you is expected.

Given the recollection of shared happiness,

can't ignore the incisions

around your handprint on my heart.

Still dripping the remembrance

of your unpredicted episodes

leaving me torn between

different men emerging from the same body.

You made it easy to walk away.

Will I ever return to witness any significant difference?

No, I will hope for the best

while laying any thoughts of

you and I together again

to rest.

Stepping Up to the Number One Spot (Love Remix)

I don't want to be the other woman.

I want to be the woman

who solely has his heart.

I don't want to taste

the residue of someone else's lips on a man.

I want to receive affection

from my one and only admirer.

I don't want to be the woman

who fantasizes about or wishes he has.

I want to be the woman he is delighted to be with.

I don't want to be the woman

he won't commit to,

but willing to receive the benefits of the relationship.

I want to be the woman

he connects with, gives his all to fully commit.

I don't want him to wish
his girl was like me.
I want him to be happy with what he has in me.

In other words, I don't want to be
the woman on the side.
He is too prideful
to admit to his unhappiness
or that woman who is here for his convenience.
Better yet, move out of my face.
Free up my space so I will be available for
the man I deserve whose priority is to chase me only.

I Wish I Knew Then What I Know Now

I remember when he uttered the words.

Mixed emotions of disbelief

and

sweet happiness

wanted to

hear

him

say

 it

again.

       He wouldn't.

      He couldn't

           face the fact

              that

    he

      was

   now

feeling

what I have always felt.

He didn't want to

answer the call

to come out

of

the field of

plucking roses.

He wanted to

keep dealing with

childish habits

by

not stopping

to savor

the

sweet fragrance

of

love.

Fooling me

into

thinking that

I should

continue to

                        wait

                for

        him.

        When he uttered

        those words,

        I was washing dishes at the sink

        after he cooked for me

        and his homeboys.

        While hoping

        that

        I

        was

         also

        washing away

                        the

                        filth

                        of

                        regret

                Thoughts of relief

                swept over me

                because

        I knew

        my investment

wasn't

in vain.

I

wanted

to

hear

those words

again

    but

        he

            knew

        he

            wasn't

                  here

                      to

                  stay.

        He

            knew

                that

        he

            was

            only

                a tenant

and

didn't

plan

on

making

a

permanent

residence

in my

heart

so

he wouldn't

say

the words

again.

O, how I needed

him

to say

the words

again

so

I

wouldn't be

broken

hearted

one other

time

because

I

blinded

myself

to the truth

that

he took

what

I

gave

with no intention

of

reciprocating...

The truth

that

I

was chasing

him

into

a fantasy

that

he

never

desired

to play

a

major role

in.

The truth

that

we were

never

made

to be

more

than

friends.

⚜

Fear of Tomorrow Without You

I don't want you here,
but when you ask to leave
I insist you stay.

I need you.
Explaining why
I am still holding on to you.
Why do I continue to smile
when sadness and disappointment
lingers around my heart
whenever you are around?

I want you to go.
Freeing myself of the misery.
Fearing the pain of life without you
keeps me from loosening my grasp.
I am not happy.

Yet being scared of starting all over again

imprisons me in your company.

Obligation has impaired my judgment

on what is best for me.

Being afraid of loneliness has stalled the break-up.

How much longer can I live with the decision

to stay in a stagnant place

not bringing joy to my face?

When will I find enough strength

to push me out of my comfort zone

with you no longer to depend on?

Embracing the unknown is not an easy move to make.

For the sake of sanity,

I must press my way.

THROUGH

I will not allow loneliness to push me back
into the arms of a man who is incapable of love.

Drama, obligations, frustrations, situations
bound your arms from…
holding me when I needed you,
reaching out when you needed me.

I tried to maneuver through.
My love wasn't enough to break through,
to keep you.
Another thorny line of promises would block my path--
the aftermath is
torn clothes, ripped skin, red tears, scorned soul.

My heart battled with my soul.
She didn't want to let you go.

My soul won the battle

couldn't take the pain anymore.

No longer grieving a loss

when it was a gain

to let go of what drained my soul to empty.

I won't allow...

A song, restaurant, poem, drink, sport or any distant memory reconnecting me to you.

Through.

I am through.

I am through with you.

Desperate for Love

You have never expressed interest
in being in a relationship with me.

Who am I
to imagine us being together?
Not realizing
too much daydreaming
can cause me to slightly confuse
fantasy with reality.

Forgetting you never came on to me.

Only seeing you desiring me.

I keep calling.
Trying to make you see
we have something special between us.

Failing to remember you never mentioned

US

in a sentence.

Daily envisioning

you and me

side-by-side.

Desperately, I want you to want me like I want you.

I stop by your house unannounced.

Give you gifts.

Nurse you when you are sick.

Cook when you are hungry.

Sex you when you are horny.

All these things I will do for you.

I need you to love me.

Exit Left

Don't fool yourself into thinking,
believing or wishing
I will stop breathing.
My world will stop turning
because you decided to burn down
this foundation we built together.
With stormy weather,
sunshine always follows.
Sometimes a rainbow will appear
the promise is still alive –
a brighter tomorrow filled with
hope, encouragement,
I can travel this road
without you.
Without any baggage called
Regret –
I should have made it work.

Pipe dream –

He will open his eyes,

realize he needs me.

Never mind all that

I'm good.

The Beginning

They say it will come when you least expect it

from someone you would have never guessed.

Blindsiding you from unbelief to euphoria.

Having you open to exploring the possibility of becoming a reality

God has not forsaken this particular desire of your heart.

A desire has ignited a beautiful friendship blossoming into whatever

He wills it.

In the midst, I feel so honored and blessed

He loved me so much it could be with you.

I wonder if I found love.

I know I found a present I love unwrapping daily

Conversations revealing the inner parts of you

pulling me further into your heart.

From the start, I was saying hi

and it turned into hearing

"I was the guy who wanted you to be my girl."

Now as adults

I wonder how I missed it.

Really doesn't matter.

At this moment, I wonder if I found love, the one.

God gave us this time to reunite

rekindling a flame you once felt

igniting a flame I never expected to experience.

Desiring to be engulfed.

Drowning in whatever you're serving.

Savoring slowly your fragrance.

Intoxicating, mesmerizing, tantalizing my intellect.

Open while trying not to second guess

if my heart hasn't deceived me again.

Have I found love?

Wondering when is the next time I will be in your arms.

It has been too long.

Keep telling myself to hold on.

Be patient.

The obligation and dedication to other matters

doesn't make me mad or jealous.

Wondering when is the next time I will be in your arms.

Staring in those chocolate drops.

Not talking much because I am staring,

savoring every inch of you.

Being next to you.

Held by you.

Brown skin wrapped in brown skin,

rich chocolate never satisfying the sweetest craving.

Never can get enough,

which is why I am lying here wondering.

Tired of imagining

Daydreaming and I'm thinking of you

Dreaming nightly about the possibility of forever

being held by you.

I wonder ...

Avoiding the Label

In that moment,

my lips want to utter

something I should feel for another.

However, entangled in my emotions,

I can't admit this sentiment isn't genuine.

Reality is nonexistent.

Yet, in this moment

I am creating and molding a saying to fit

what was never meant to be.

Casually, I let the music play

the same tune you hear in the movies,

the love stories, soap operas with the sappy ending.

"We belong together and you know that I am . . .."

No, I am not right.

This is all wrong.

Rewriting the script

Professing I am in love,

not with the man

God blessed me from above,

but with the feeling of being in love.

Being a part of a never-ending intimate embrace.

Pretending my heart beats for you.

Willing to take this journey with you—

A path unknown far away from my home.

Destiny does not await me.

Warning me, I have chosen to seek my own understanding.

Impatient,

tired of the clock ticking.

Granting your wish, dream, and fantasy.

Creating a false truth,

I need your last name to put a period

on this seemingly never-ending run-on chapter of my life.

Being called someone's wife is the fulfillment I seek.

Tired of the sucking of teeth

followed by the fake laugh asking me,

"How come you ain't got no man?"

Willing to shout from the mountaintop.

Post pics on Instagram.

Change my status on Facebook.

Tag him on every picture so they can look and see

be proud of me.

Momma, aunty, cousins, and homies,

I didn't let another good man slip away.

None of them ask if I prayed for you.

No, they elated

I stopped waiting.

Anticipating me saying, yes, I do.

Ask God to bless the mess later.

Gotta escape the label of being alone.

Forcing a house to be a home.

Never built to last.

Sinking in sand

beneath the standard.

A standard sent down from Heaven

with specific instructions,

promises guaranteeing

life more abundantly.

Surely that doesn't apply to matrimony.

God is taking too long!

Blinded by all the wedding rings,

It seems everyone has a boo thang except me.

That one last train has stopped

and I am getting on without His permission.

I am missing God's best.

Faithless in the process.

Determined to avoid the label

of being single.

Part Five

9 - 11

World Inspirations

Invisible to Nonexistent

He said, "They don't see me."

    "They can't see me."

My reply, three years later is…

You think they are really afraid of you?

They are not trying to see you

Turning a blind eye . . .

Ignoring the behavior.

Setting you up for failure—

More write-ups lead to suspensions.

More suspensions lead to expulsion.

Eventually, you won't see the point of an education.

Dropping out of school

to only end up some O.G.'s fool,

doing his dirty work.

Never do you learn your lesson.

In and out of the juvenile court system

They see you.

Crossing their fingers,

hoping you will stay locked into the image

of another black face overcrowding federal prisons.

Erasing your parents' wishes

of you graduating from college.

Threatening to take over

what society says will never be yours.

All this time they are watching you.

Planning to capitalize on your demise.

You think they can't see you.

They're trying to carry out their plan

to erase your existence.

9 - 11

Tears well up in my eyes

When I think about those who lost their lives

Someone wanted to prove a point.

Revenge and superiority is the reasoning

Daughters lost mothers....

Sons lost fathers...

Sisters, brothers, husbands, wives …

and other friends and relatives

Who can only be relived

   through memories and dreams.

Hopes to see them again

isn't enough to dull the pain.

Heartache spreads

We in turn send our own

to make the ultimate sacrifice

while leaving behind family and friends

who cling on to hope they will return.

Now on their turf, we return the favor.

The vendetta has been accomplished...

To what cost...

More blood mixed with tears pollutes

streams, rivers, and oceans

Effluence of cries --

sorrow, hatred, disappointment echoes loudly.

Why can't our government see

they are ruining families on both sides...

... Due to pride

Need to fix the mess

Keeps permeating into more families.

Destroying them like stage four cancer.

Nations can't stand our condition of Megalomania.

This great nation can't even fix problems

in our own terrain.

Yet we transport many into enemy territory

or in any country

to be their enforcer or promising hope.

What a joke when . . .

Our schools suffer . . .

Hunger is an everyday language of many . . .

Families are no longer functional . . .

Mommy and daddy aren't always home . . .

They have to protect our freedom,

Neglecting their own.

Returning to the unknown

Life isn't always the same when returning home . . .

Sacrifices are forgotten

Jobs are hard to land

The endless cycle continues

Started because of his resentment

Praying it will end soon.

Don't Call It a Comeback

Never ever say there isn't enough time.

When I single handedly

Defied the odds

Smashing hopes and dreams

Shocking The Garden

in 3.1 seconds.

You thought it was playtime

Basketball arena turned playground

Chuckling and laughing

Believed you bagged a win

Ready to shake hands,

casually say good effort to the losers.

Didn't care if there was less than 20 seconds left.

The game isn't over until the buzzer sounds

Until then . . .

I am determined to leave with a W etched in my crown

Punks settle for L's

Give up before the bell.

School isn't over.

Matter of fact, I am about to teach you all a lesson

On how to win.

Don't call this a comeback.

Always envisioned I would be the one celebrating in the end.

Taunting you all.

You really thought this was the beginning of you winning it all?

Determined to shatter your hope

Refusing to hear another fan yell or disrespect one of the greatest.

Give me the ball

Shocking the crowd with my shot from downtown.

Spike Lee, I can't hear you now. (Drop the music)

Snatch your cookies

Really your pride

Embarrassment is an understatement.

You didn't really want it

Falling to the floor

Crying for a foul

While I shock the crowd

with another three.

You want to blame this loss on me

Your boy couldn't drain two free throws.

Your other boy couldn't even bank the rebonded shot.

Getting got doesn't feel so hot

Hands on the head.

Fans in the stands

bowing in agony

Defeat is so heartless.

Victory causes me to pound my chest

Proved again I am the best.

Bring Back ...

Bring back the days
      of the original Twin Towers
Teams that had power
      that wouldn't fade
      until after two or three or six
      championships

Teams with stars that were
     accompanied by a supporting cast

Magic, Worthy, Scott, Jabbar, Green

Olajuwon, Maxwell, Smith, Cassell, Horry

Jordan, Pippen, Grant, Kerr, Armstrong

Let's go back to the days of dominance

  Teams that played hard

    all season

      not waiting for the playoffs

        To make a statement

          Protecting the reputation

            of winning was an oath

              no one broke.

Teams that won back-to-back

  Due to staying with the players

    that got them there.

  Acquiring players who

    would keep the flame

    torching other teams to a crisp

        No one is getting in the way

        of another championship

Let's go back to when it was easier to be a fan.

  I saw the face of the same man

    for years to come.

  Contracts lasted longer

    for the starting five and

      the sixth man.

Players weren't hopping teams

    chasing a championship

    Developing a team to that caliber

        was the objective...

            And it happened...

Patience was a virtue

    that existed in the league

Let's resurrect a pure love for the game

    Winning

        Etching my name as one of the bests

           Might not have won a championship

             Wasn't going to jump ship

               Just to have bling on my finger

            Content with playing the game

              People knowing my name in my town

            that I built

             sustained

        Never will abandon my city

        LOYALTY

Does anyone know what that means?

My hoop dream is to wake up

    to yesterday

Don't see them revamping

    the system anytime soon.

    Too busy giving techs for questioning the refs.

    Deciding what should be divided between

        the owners and the players.

    Tired of watching the shenanigans.

        When will a foul ever truly be a foul

           without you taking a bow in the end.

Since you can't take me back

Please answer my plea to bring it back . . .

I won't ever abandon you ...

Maybe that is why you won't change

I guess we will meet again ...

during the playoffs, of course ...

My Job Description

With my hands,

I carefully mold clay

That will one day

Pave the way...

With their major corporations

Inspiring music

Stylistic fashion trends.

With my mouth,

I speak life

Into the next generation

Who will soon...

Find a cure for an incurable disease

Rescue a battered woman in dire need

Have sports' fans jumping out of their seats.

With the gift to inspire,

I will lift many children higher

Than any negative statistic that says

They will never make it.

Yes, the road will be rough

But they will remember to never give up.

You ask what exactly do I do?

I teach.

My Gifts

Christmas comes early for me...

Every year

right around August

I am blessed with

100 or more gifts

that bless me

every day.

In the midst of

laughs, tears, screams, rants, debates, cheers,

encouraging you to face your fears,

pushing you to maximize your potential

my heart is always grateful

to experience

these blessed gifts

that will leave

my presence in June,

while leaving a lasting impression

on my heart

forever.

As your teacher,

I am still learning, growing

Thank you for showing me

How I can do better.

Eternally grateful

for you being such

awesome, beautiful presents!

Hate Won't Win

There are not enough
      not enough good cops
      who stop the bad ones.
As sad as the reality
      some wanted to be hooded.
Wearing a white sheet isn't as popular.
Wearing blue with a badge
      covers up and muffles the truth.
You never wanted to serve and protect.
Your hate is a generational curse
      lingering, hovering, hollering these niggas ain't free.
Never deserved the right to be.
Stole your family's way of life from you
      when we broke those chains.
Escaped with knowledge and power to rebel
      against the lies, we are beneath you.
With conviction, we repeatedly remind you we have
      a right to life, liberty and the pursuit of happiness.

You had to do what was necessary.

You set that bounty high.

Getting to the point

    it didn't matter if we don't fit the description.

As long as we fit the race,

    we would serve as your slave until death.

Four hundred years later,

We watch the same horror film.

Too many wrongful convictions

    to be turned over with a boy in a man's body.

Stripped of his innocence.

Sent back to the world to be a productive citizen

    while watching my other brothers be harassed

    eventually gunned down.

You fear your life now.

Afraid we know who we are.

Afraid we will remember you screwed us

    over and over and over.

Still, we marched, prayed and hoped.

Protested, sang of strength and glory of

    how one day we can tell the story, hate couldn't win.

Your vile ignorance is sin.

We're actually better than you.

We built businesses, towns, and villages sustaining economic freedom, eventually you would burn down to the ground.

Yet, we kept growing,

       knowing eventually our Lord will see us through.

Gaining opportunities

Equal representation

Changing laws

We won't settle for a loss or lose heart because

       another white sheet is silencing another black king on the streets.

       locking up another victim of the system who profits more than

       rehabilitate souls.

We will continue to reform the system.

Even when you ain't trying to hear ...

When your thinking is so unclear ...

Rationalizing deadly force when you see a lynching.

Can't fathom you can't get rid of us.

We are free.

Royalty,

Building kingdoms

Free of this hypocrisy and ideology, hate will win.

We will champion an anthem mobilizing the troops to fight again with weapons, you can't imagine.

Tearing down strongholds.

Destroying your mantles.

More of us orchestrating a symphony, harmonies of unity

Determined hate won't win.

Because of Them, We Can

I am the legacy

My grandmother prayed for.

Sitting in a room that was once inaccessible.

Enjoying the fruits of their labor.

Protests, marches, rallies, sit-ins

Interrupted by ripped skin due to dog bites and fire truck hoses

Limped away with bruises from the constant

collision with bats and night sticks

Bricks shattering their windows.

Burning crosses on their lawns

Death threats

Bombs killing the innocent

Bullets shot to intimidate

Paralyze the fight.

I am the beacon of hope.

The light shining as a testimony

I have overcome it.

Still have to endure some hardship.

But it won't stop me from appreciating

what my ancestors did for me

Not caring about being labeled nerd or geek.

Getting mine

Some people aren't alive

Died to ensure this right was a reality and not an unattainable dream

So who am I to waste it?

Excellence flows through me

Mediocrity is beneath me.

I am more than an athlete.

I am the heartbeat of those who wanted better for me

Didn't let Jim Crow stop what God promised.

I am a trailblazer in my own right

Nevertheless, I don't forget their fight

created a pathway

For me to determine my destiny

Refusing to fall victim to the identities

Stereotypical of my people

Dropping out of the school system

Overcrowding the prisons

Impregnating many women

or

having several baby daddies

Stuck on the corner with no goals or ambition

Or collecting a check from the system

because I am too lazy to provide the best for my family.

There is no excuse for me to emulate what is expected

when my people were inventors, professors, politicians, doctors, scientists, lawyers, actors, and millionaires,

in a world where they weren't accepted.

Constantly being defiled with

"Sit in the back or give up your seat."

"You can't lodge in my facility."

"No, you can't go to school with us."

"We don't serve your kind."

"Know your place boy."

When there wasn't a road built for them,

 they created one.

There are no excuses when I have all the tools.

Examples who broke all the rules and laws.

Greatness isn't restricted to pale skin.

I am a torch bearer.

I have a responsibility to go higher.

Defy gravity.

Achieve greater than those who went before me.

Overjoyed, the mortification and torment was worth it.

Their tears and blood weren't wasted.

Their fight wasn't in vain.

The victory isn't tainted.

I am their hope, their dream, their reality and their legacy.

Encore

I applaud
YOU
today.

YOU
are not letting
the sweat,

tears,

and

blood of your ancestors

go to waste.

YOU
refuse to settle for
mediocrity
when it comes to
your destiny.

Whether or not

YOU

realize it,

the ones who marched,

participated in sit-ins,

protested while singing hymns

would be overjoyed.

YOU

only focus

your eyes

to see

A' and B's as a testament

of

your personal best,

acknowledging excellence

lows through

your veins.

People suffered torment

and

death threats.

But

not in vain...

Now

their seeds of equality

won't be uprooted due to a

barren field.

YOU

have flourished into a bountiful harvest

a man would have to travel for years to see.

YOU

have taken advantage of the best education,

maximizing your potential

Magnet programs, Honors, and AP level courses.

YOU

haven't forgotten the sacrifice

of

either some of

your ancestors' life

or

pain from dog bites,

ripped skinned due to fire truck hoses

or

bruises from the constant collision

with bats and night sticks.

YOU

are determined to keep paving the road

they

started, focused on preparing now.

Achieving positive goals

like honor roll or being valedictorian.

Thirsting for knowledge

reading books and googling to enrich.

Pursuing a future career

   that will elevate the future generations

to more and new heights of achievement

like being President.

They wish they could witness

the wave of brown hands rising at different peaks.

YOU

want the teacher to acknowledge your intellect.

Studying to show yourself approved is the trophy

gleaming brightly in the case.

All stop to marvel at it from the front of the school.

Asking questions for clarification or posing "what ifs"

is only the polish erasing the dullness.

All these actions

YOU

execute unconsciously or consciously thanking

those who paved the way

by paying a high price to ensure

your equal rights are a reality

and not an unattainable dream.

About the Author

Rian N. Jenkins' has been in love with writing since sixth grade. Close to thirty years, she has inspired, entertained, and educated many through poetry, novellas, journalism, and spoken word performances. Finally, she can add author to her resume.

Along with being a gifted writer, she has been a devoted and passionate educator for almost seventeen years.

She is the mother of Joshua.

In her spare time, she loves to watch sports, especially football, thrift, and read a lot of YA lit she shares with her students and the world via YouTube.

To learn more information about her or how to book her for a performance, author visit, or writer's workshop, visit her website, www.riannjenkins.com.